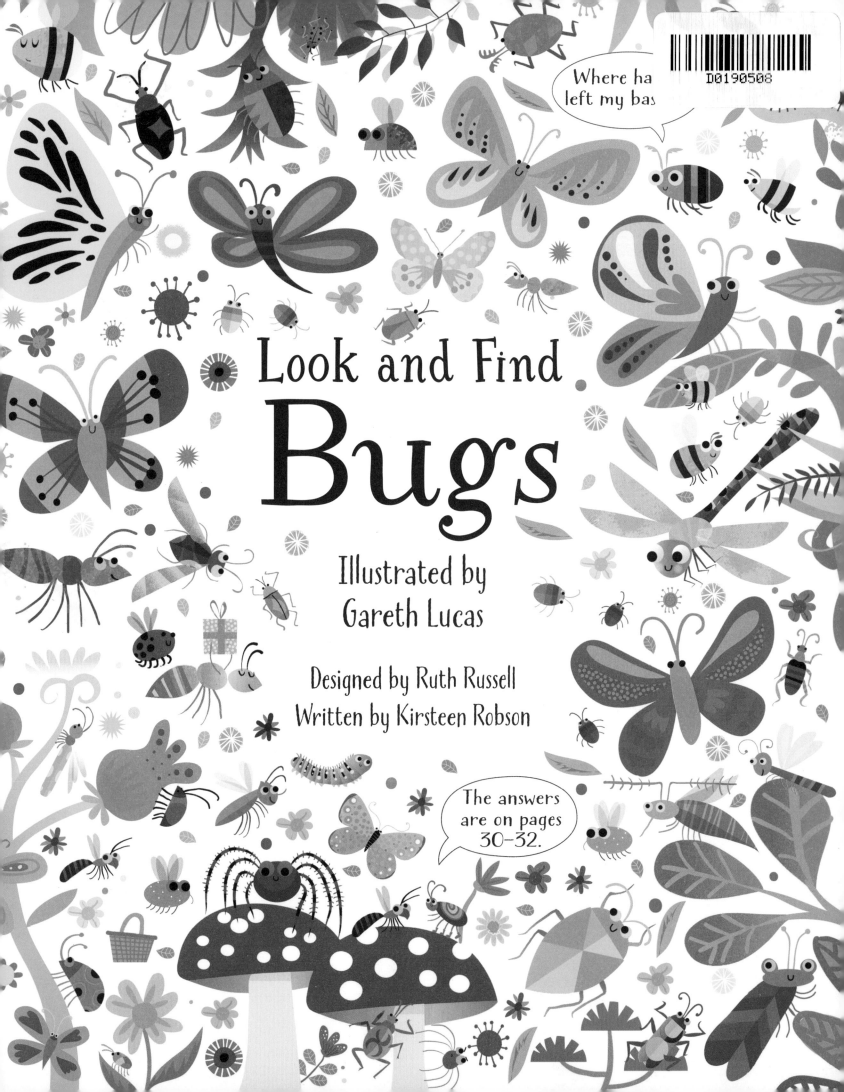

Look and Find
Bugs

Illustrated by
Gareth Lucas

Designed by Ruth Russell
Written by Kirsteen Robson

Where ha
left my bas

The answers
are on pages
30-32.

22

ANSWERS

Cover

The blue bee is on page 1.

1

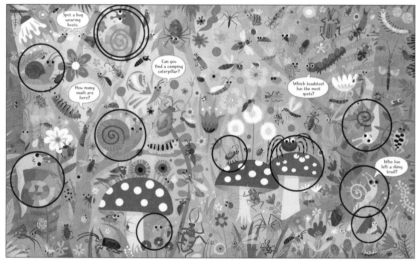

There are 7 snails.

2-3

4-5

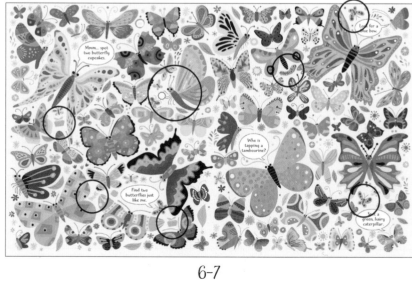

6-7

8-9

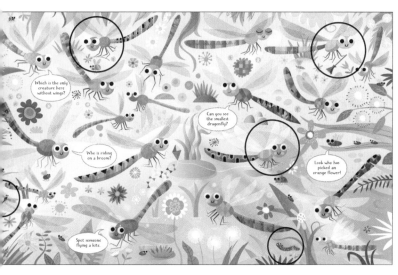

10-11

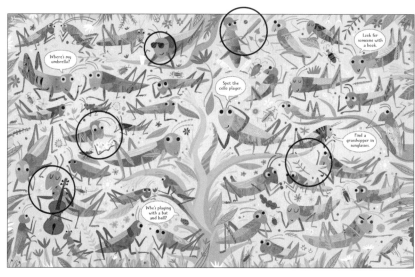

12-13

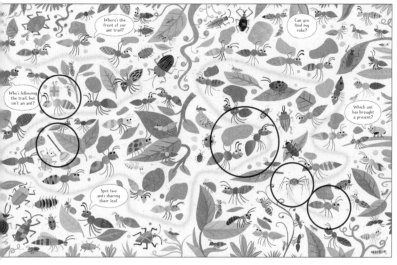

14-15

There are 6 caterpillars.

16-17

18-19

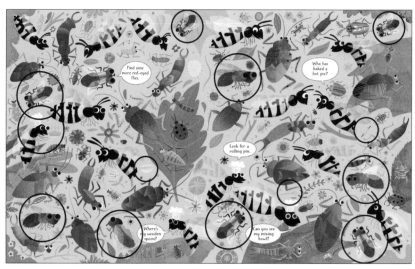

20-21

31

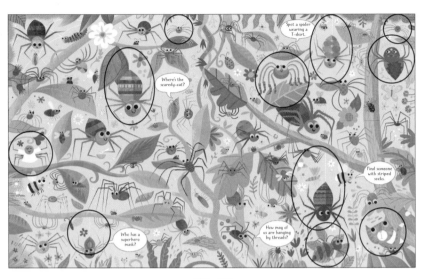

7 spiders are hanging by threads.   22–23

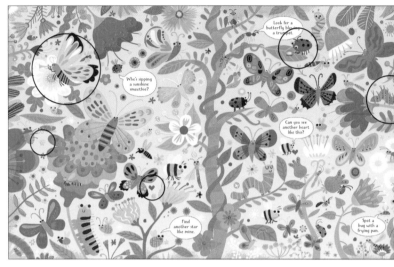

24–25

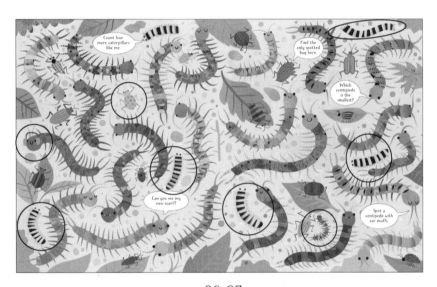

26–27

28–29

First published in 2018 by Usborne Publishing Ltd, Usborne House, 83–85 Saffron Hill, London, EC1N 8RT, England. www.usborne.com
Copyright © 2018 Usborne Publishing Ltd. The name Usborne and the devices ♕ ⊕ are Trade Marks of Usborne Publishing Ltd. All rights reserved.
No part of this publication may be reproduced, stored in a retrieval system, or transmitted in any form or by any means, electronic, mechanical,
photocopying, recording or otherwise, without the prior permission of the publisher. UKE. Printed in China.